Creative Cash

10 Steps to Creating More Profit in Your Beautiful Business

WWW.JOELLEBYRNE.COM

COPYRIGHT

Contents

About the Author

Before we go any further and we start to really make headway on your biz, I better tell you a bit about myself, so you know who the hell I am!

I'm Joelle, long time entrepreneur and strategist. I help women like you to get more money out of your existing creative business and turn your passion into profits.

Here's the short version:

Having worked for over a decade in the public sector and being a serial entrepreneur on the side, exchanging my time for money, I decided it was time to start sharing my knowledge in a different way. (Plus, I really wanted to spend some more time with the man I married and the small human I made! Sound familiar?)

Working online for entrepreneurs, bloggers and business owners for the last 3 years has given me a really unique insight into what works (and what doesn't work!) to make a creative business rack up the cash.

This business began when having conversations over coffee with small-biz-owner friends about how they could generate more income in their business. This led to acquaintances and then strangers asking for similar advice... and all of them were achieving awesome results!

So, I figured it was time to reach out and help more and more women to lead their ultimate lives and generate more from their beautiful, unique businesses! Sometimes, a new perspective is all you need!

I want to teach you (as an exceptional woman!) that, in order to make more money in your business, you don't need to create more hours in the day.

YOU don't have to work harder, longer or faster. Just smarter. And I'm so pleased you chose me to teach you how!

Jo
XOXO

JoelleByrne.com

Start Here
Because It's the Beginning

Right now, whatever your small business sells, whether it's handmade products you individually craft, or services that you provide (like coaching or holistic therapies), your business is probably based on exchanging your time for money. It's sad because that is very much like employment in some ways. You go to work and in return you get a salary.

But you didn't start your business to work like that did you?

And you and I both know that it isn't physically possible for you to sell more than so many time-slots in one day or to create more of your designs than you're currently producing - there are still only 24 hours in the day.

But it is possible to sell more of what you already create and to diversify where some of the income in your business actually comes from. The more income streams you have, the higher your turnover and the more customers you can reach.

When you stop believing that you need to exchange time for money, or at least some of the time, you can begin to generate revenue from streams that manage themselves. This is called passive income, and it's one of the best ways to get more cash into your existing business.

So here I am with a plan for you. This book is jam packed full of ideas you might want to consider that will help you sell more AND generate more revenue without physically doing too much additional work. It's got to be a winner, right?

So, how do you think those making huge amounts of revenue in their business are actually doing it? I promise you, they have not got a time machine to create more hours in the day and they don't have some magic tonic that makes them work at a thousand miles an hour!

It doesn't matter what you do, whether it's life or business - success is not a secret, it's a system. It's a series of strategically designed steps that take you from desire to goal – over and over again. And when it comes to business, it really doesn't matter what you're selling, as long as you have a well-considered strategy and plan, you'll make it.

There are 3 ways that women running 6 and 7 figure empires are doing just that. These women are JUST LIKE YOU! They probably started their business in their living room, just like you did.

You can invite more money into your business by applying the step by step principals in this book, which will help you to go from "just enough" to "plenty". If you take all the steps and implement what works for your business model of course.

This journey will teach you to:

- See the value of goals, plans and strategy for YOUR measure of success – no one else's

- Make more real sales and introduce additional active income streams to your business

- Implement passive income streams that see you making sales when you're sleeping – really!

It's split into 3 main parts:

1. **Business Fundamentals**

This is where we talk about the backbone of your business. Without these 4 things in place working for you, don't bother doing the rest. They're that important to business.

2. New Income Streams

This is where I'm going to throw some epic ideas at you so you can start generating more income into your business. We'll talk passive and active income streams. Implement one or more to see huge results in your monthly turnover.

3. Smart Work & Marketing

Finally, we'll pull it all together with some smart marketing talk. Nothing complex, just a series of simple steps to get you selling ALL of your new income streams on the regular.

So, there you have it. This book is designed to be an overview, an introduction, a value-driven guide that gets your own creative juices flowing to create more money in your business. I'm so looking forward to working with you and building your empire, as you see it!

Business Fundamentals

To create more money, you need to have the basics right. Steps 1 to 4 take you through the business basics that, even on their own, will increase your business turnover and help you to create a more profitable, sustainable business.

Your Measure of Success

The first thing you need to do on your road to success is decide what that actually is! Your measure of success is what success looks like to you – it's as simple as that.

What is Success?

There's one answer to this question: success is entirely your own perception. We apply the term "success" so liberally and to so many endeavours in our lives; from the amount of money we make to our careers and our families – even the house we live in! But what I consider successful may be way too low a standard for someone else.

Your measure of success depends entirely on:

- Your experiences of life so far
- Your ambitions for yourself and your family
- Your motives
- Your wants and desires

You can only be successful if you know what you actually want. By measuring the outcomes of your achievements against the goals you set and where you WANT to be, you can determine what success looks like to you and when you get there.

The only rules for success that I will strongly suggest you set for yourself is that success is incremental. If I'm sat here in my mansion and driving my top of the range car (I'm not by the way, but I will be!) success might look very different to me than it does to the single mom living in a one-bedroom apartment. And that's not to say that the apartment isn't the absolute epitome of success for that individual. That could've been her big goal! Especially when you consider that she may have once been homeless or had countless awful things occur in her life.

Success is about what you want it to be. Who's to say what YOUR success should look like?

And also, who's to say that success stops there? That you've reached the top of your game once you get to that initial goal?

Incrementally speaking, if you've made it from living on the streets to your gorgeous little flat, then who's to say that the mansion isn't the next stop? If you want that of course!

But it doesn't have to be!

And who's business is it anyway but yours? Both in whether or not it has anything to do with anyone else but also, it's your damn business, right? It's your name above the door.

Who's to say you should be striving for that multi-million-pound life? Why not just a comfortable 3-bed semi? Who is to say, but you?

So, for starters, let's get rid of the mindset that success is for other people. It's not. Success depends entirely upon what YOU WANT IT TO BE. Not what society thinks it is. And although that's a lesson all on its own, it needs saying here, because it's important for you to understand that these keys to financial abundance don't apply to someone else; they're yours to take, implement and profit from as well.

Your Mindset

I'm part of a number of all female entrepreneur Facebook groups, as most of you will be if you've jumped on the business bandwagon head first! And I've noticed a recent trend in lots of women having a serious inability to believe in themselves. Each week I see similar posts on my feed about fear of failure, dealing with negativity and roadblocks that women are actually creating themselves. So, I got to thinking; what the hell is holding you back?

Over the last decade, loads of surveys have been completed about business and specifically, the divide of the sexes within entrepreneurship. Even terms like "grabbing business by the balls" personifies business in men's clothing! These surveys tell us all sorts of things, and some of it is certainly good news, but not all.

As females in business we are on the rise, whoop! But still, only 30% of all US businesses are majority female owned. I'm not mincing my words with how I feel about that. It's absolute shit!

We should be breaking even by now ladies!

"In the UK between 2008 and 2011, women accounted for an unprecedented 80% of the new self-employed" (fist-pump!) But still, we can't get the

edge over those pesky blokes (we love 'em really!)
(Source: <u>Prowess</u>)

I love a good statistic, so I really delved into this. During my research one of the main, stand-out facts, that bellowed at me from the page was this:

"In every single economy included (in one particular study back in 2013), women have lower capabilities perception than men. In every region, women have, on average, a greater level of fear of failure than men." (Source: <u>Prowess</u>)

This tells me one thing; that it's our own fault that we're not on a 50/50 split with the guys! Erm…..

Our own fears and insecurities are making us anxious to try because "failure" is there hiding in the background like some weird Grim Reaper. (Creepy much?)

We're building our own walls, in addition to the already existing fences that we have to leap! For women, this takes self-deprecating to a whole different level – to absolute, unadulterated, self-destruction.

And it has to stop.

Despite some of these rubbish statistics and the odds being stacked against us, there is proof that women who ARE in business and DO challenge their own fears are more successful than men:

"Companies helmed by women entrepreneurs had 13% higher revenues than those run by men and finished 9% above the average for all entrepreneurs surveyed." (source: Forbes)

So what?

So, my question is, what the hell are we going to do about it? Which women are we going to be? The scared or the successful? This quote from Skylar Grey sums it up for me:

"Your personal life, your professional life, and your creative life are all intertwined. I went through a few very difficult years where I felt like a failure. But it was actually really important for me to go through that. Struggle, for me, is the most inspirational thing in the world at the end of the day – as long as you treat it that way."

Just like Skylar, I believe that we should be making a difference in every aspect of our lives by simply switching one fundamental part of our female make-up – self-worth! Believing that we're capable of more, shutting down the doubts and fears, telling imposter syndrome to take a hike and replacing those negative thoughts with positivity, gratitude and pure damn self-belief!

Those of you who are mothers will be able to relate to that feeling when you come out of hospital with the new human you made. The sense of elation is amazing (before the reality of parenting and sleepless nights kick in!) But the thought of all of those other women, before and after you, who have done just what you did! That resounds so loudly! Wow! We rock! Revelling in the miracle of what women are truly capable of is one of the best things, on a personal level, about becoming a mom! We're a force to be reckoned with.

Let's look at what we actually do:

- We're capable of running a family and a business or career
- Manage life when it's crazy and all of the responsibilities
- Raise children and support husbands, partners, friends and family members who need us
- Look after parents and family members when they're no longer able to do things for themselves
- We REMEMBER EVERYTHING and are usually the ones in the home that organise what needs to happen and when!

- Balance tasks with an innate sense of prioritising; we remember the bread when there's a disaster and know what will make a loved one feel better when something goes a bit wrong

We're pretty flaming awesome! Why aren't we applying that awesome superpower to our business?

So, having recognised that the fear can come from overwhelm and the unknown, perhaps it's time to tackle that head on? There are far too many "resources" out there that claim to teach us everything we need to know about being successful. I've fallen for the same click bait myself; too many times! Pinterest has become my best friend and worst enemy in providing traffic and ideas for my home and business, but then distracting me with all the amazing "ultimate guide to business...." Pins I end up procrastinating over. Which can instil fear because we're not doing "all the things".

But recognising that the huge amounts of different tools, techniques, tips and tricks available to entrepreneurs aren't applicable to everyone, especially you, is a great start. Recognising that you can't learn and implement everything is the next step. You can have a stupendously successful business by focussing your energy on the essentials that create the fundamental makeup of your business, all of which we'll deal with, in this book:

- Access – Can people find you? Are you confusing them?
- Service – Are you providing the service you set out to provide? Whatever that is?
- Customers – Do you have them and are you making connections in a real way in order to find them?
- Revenue – Are you making money? If you're not, you're not running a business, are you? What are people actually paying you for?

All you need to do is invest some time and belief in yourself, and you really can't go far wrong.

Setting Goals, You'll Actually Achieve

So, your first task is goal setting. Don't you dare yawn! Because the truth of the matter is; if you don't know where you're going then:

- How will you get there?
- How will you know what "there" even looks like?
- How will you know if you're already there? What if you've already made it?

Imagine goal setting and planning like a holiday. If you're going somewhere to catch some rays, take in the scenery or just spending some down-time with your family, then you usually know the following:

- Why you're going - because if you didn't, what's the point of going in the first place?
- What you want to do - because if you didn't, you might end up in a sea side resort when you actually wanted to go sightseeing?
- Where you're going - because if you didn't, would you actually go anywhere and how would you know if you'd arrived?

- How you're getting there - because if you didn't, it would be pretty chaotic, and you'd probably get lost - a lot!
- When you're going - because if you didn't, how would your other half know to turn up? How would you know which flight to catch?

Get my drift?

So, even though setting goals and making plans might seem a bit woo-woo; it's actually essential to the success of any trip, project or business. Without knowing what you're doing, you're just fumbling around in the dark trying to achieve something, but you don't even know what that something is.

Today then, I want you to think about and write down the answers to the following questions:

- How much time do you want to spend in your business?
- What can you realistically commit to and what do you actually want to do?
- How do you really feel about your business success and what does that success look like? - is it a certain amount of money being made? How much?
- What would your ideal business look like?

- How many sales are you making each week/month/year?
- How many social media followers do you have? Does that even matter?
- Are there publications you'd like to appear in?
- Do you want to speak at events? Where?
- Are you an influencer in your niche?
- Do you have employees?
- Do you have loads of holidays and time with your family?
- Are you retiring your partner?
- When would you like to achieve these goals?
- What's a good time scale? Why that timescale? Why that date?

Setting Your Why

Tony Robbins says….

"Setting goals is the first step in turning the invisible into the visible"

This is a super popular quote, used time and time again across the internet. But what it fails to capture is the rest of the story. So, you got yourself a goal, a destination? Good for you! But like we've already said, that is just the beginning. It is not a magic wand which will magically turn you into a millionaire basking on a beach, or suddenly have you living in your dream home.

The reason why most people fail to complete or be successful at goal setting in general, is because their goals are empty. There is no why. Essentially, without it, you're off to a false start.

Without a reason your goals become empty vessels. They become easily forgotten, passionless and without gravity.

For each and every goal you set for yourself, you need to attach two fundamental and emotional elements:

- your why
- your why not

Why?

Linking your resolutions or goals, for business and your personal life, to a reason that hits you somewhere in your gut, on an emotional level, is the next step. Your why needs to resonate with you and make something happen in your gut. Like lighting a fire under your butt; a real, "makes me wanna cry I'm so excited" reason.

Without that, it is unlikely that you will drive significant change because you have no "why"; No real reason to change. There is no primal instinct that is the "higher power" that you'll turn to when it gets tough. And it will get tough, there is no doubt.

Why Not?

Your why nots are as important as your "why's". They're like the other side of the wall. Without these, you're on unstable ground to say the least. Now, this isn't about being negative, certainly not. But it is about being realistic. Your why nots should be what will happen and/or how you will feel if you don't meet your goal.Thinking happy thoughts and driving toward those goals with an emotional attachment will give your entire goal more weight; more fibre. With a "why not" added to it, it's like super charging those reasons and being chased by a monster toward your goals and away from failure to meet them.

What do I mean?

Here's the step-by-step:

- Sit quietly with a blank piece of paper and write down your goals – don't think about how you'll get to them, just what you really want.
- Split them into personal and business, health and wellbeing, etc.
- When you're done, annotate those goals with a single word or short sentence describing the emotions that you feel when you think about achieving that goal.
- Then add your why. Why do you want to achieve that specific goal? Where did it come from? Follow your thoughts back to the origin of the goal and question yourself.
- Now add your why nots. What will happen if you don't meet that goal? How will it make you feel? What emotions does that bring up?
- Go back, make sense of it and write it out. There are your goals, your why's and your why nots.

There is your solid plan to achieving those goals!

Transfer it to your planner and you're on your way.

Now compare how you feel about your goals versus how you felt about them on 1st January last year when you made some resolution that you probably didn't keep. Different right?

The links that you make have to be completely personal in order to have more impact, no matter how silly they seem. These are for you, not everyone else.

What makes your heart sing or your stomach flip and therefore will be the driver of change for you?

Your goals need to be more than just a wish on a page; they need to create an emotional reaction that reminds you why you want to reach it, and what will happen if you don't. Your life, your business, your everything are no good stagnating. You need to drive forward, and you are the difference between making more money and not.

Your Plan; Your Map

Someday is not a day of the week.

A goal without a plan is just a wish.

A dream written down with a DATE becomes a goal. A goal broken down into STEPS becomes a plan. A plan backed by ACTION makes your dreams come true.

Great quotes, right? You get the message.

You've identified what you really want. Whether that be to earn a million, spend more quality time with your family or buy your dream home, it doesn't matter.

You know your why; what is really driving this decision to make change. You've written all this down.

Now it's time to get specific and decide how you're going to get there.

A big goal can be scary all by itself. But if you break it down it becomes manageable; achievable; attainable.

So, something that you can do now, and add to as you create ideas through reading this book is:

- Think about when you want to achieve your goals by (also with a why attached to it – why do you want to achieve it by then?)
- Create a plan of action that breaks it down, step by step into bite sized chunks
- Celebrate each milestone. No matter how small the step is, it's forward, toward the goal. That's worth celebrating!

Make an action plan for each goal you've set. Make the conscious decision to break down the big scary goal into manageable, actionable steps that aren't scary at all. And do them. Without this step in the process, you're still flailing around. There is no system in place to take you from A to B, which still means you're lost. It's not productive and won't get you far if you try and do this without a plan.

Oh, and don't overwhelm yourself either. Be realistic. We're not going to be millionaires next week – but we could be in 3 years' time! With a plan and good action backing it up – that is absolutely possible!

Firm Your Focus

There are other things you can do to build a fundamental backbone to your business. This simple but ridiculously effective technique NEVER FAILS and will improve EVERYTHING about your business and how much it makes. This is also the most common mistake that entrepreneurs and business owners make in the first 12 month of running their business.

What is this faux-pas?

Thinking you need to market to everyone and be everywhere! Not niching down. Not getting specific.

This could be a fundamental flaw that you've fallen into too? Business basics are at the core of how we do things and why some women are successful, and others never quite make it. This is one of the most important things you can take away to your business.

So, let's Niche Down:

One of the biggest reasons I hear women talk about not making sales is because they're trying to be something to everyone. Something they're not.

At first it does seem like the best thing to do - literally sell anything to anyone who shows an interest! But, unfortunately, that's just not going to get you very far, very fast. I promise! I've done it.... and failed! Lots of times! *(What can I say? I just don't learn first time round!)*

What is a Niche?

Your "niche market" is literally the nook where your business sits and it's the most comfortable and suitable place to be when it comes to business! It's so important to ensuring you're making sales in your business because it's your speciality - what you're really good at!

niche
/niːʃ,nɪtʃ/ ◄»

noun

1. a shallow recess, especially one in a wall to display a statue or other ornament.
   "each niche holding a shepherdess in Dresden china"
   synonyms: recess, alcove, nook, cranny, slot, slit, hollow, bay, cavity, cubbyhole, pigeonhole, opening, aperture; mihrab
   "in a niche in the wall is a statue of St John"

2. a comfortable or suitable position in life or employment.
   "he is now head chef at a leading law firm and feels he has found his niche"
   synonyms: ideal position, calling, vocation, métier, place, function, job, slot, opportunity
   "he feels he has found his niche in life"

adjective

1. denoting or relating to products, services, or interests that appeal to a small, specialized section of the population.
   "other companies in this space had to adapt to being niche players"

verb

1. place (something) in a niche.
   "these elements were niched within the shadowy reaches"

By niching down and getting super specific about WHAT you sell and WHO you sell it to, you're able to make real connections with customers who really WANT and NEED your services.

Your "niche market" is so important to ensuring you're making sales in your business. A niche is a speciality. It relates to products, services, or interests that appeal to a small, specific section of the population. If you say your product is for everyone then the sad truth bomb is; it probably appeals to no one :(If you're trying to sell to everyone then you are very likely selling to no-one at all. By reducing the circle of people you're trying to reach you'll make more sales because you're targeting your ideal client. In this way, you can speak directly to them, make a connection and make that all-important sale.

Here's a great example –

Your oven is on the blink. It's been heating things up but intermittently cutting out.

Who are you going to contact?

Your gas guy because it's a gas oven?

Or the LG Oven Man who's advert you saw last week? You remember he specialises in LG ovens over 5 years old that are on the blink. And he lives locally too.

Who would you choose?

Your audience are looking to buy a solution to a problem OR a desire that you can satisfy.

You need to know who those people are, what they do, what they spend and all their little quirks! Know this and you know your audience. Know your audience and you speak directly to them. Speak to them on a personal, real and connective level and there is your sale. Over and over again.

Your Ideal Client (Avatar)

Start by thinking about who already buys your offer or who you would like to buy your products or services. Sometimes your ideal client is YOU! Think carefully about this person, as they become your "avatar". An avatar is a description of your ideal buyer. Consider the following:

- Male or female
- Age range
- Location - live/work
- Other interests
- Occupation
- Income level
- Family makeup
- Their home, friends, social life
- Where they hang out – virtually and physically
- Blogs/books/magazines they read
- Biggest bugbears
- What else they spend their hard-earned cash on when they're not buying from you?

Most importantly, think about what their "pain point" is and what problem you're solving for them. Give that person a name too!

You can also think closely about your niche itself. Create a statement for yourself that tells anyone reading it exactly who you are, what you do and who you do it for. This statement should tell me:

- What you sell - a product, an offer, a solution, a lifestyle choice?
- What problem do you solve for your customers?
- Who does your product help?
- How do you sell it - what's your unique selling point? What makes you, you?
- Why is your product different?

Once you've done this, any promotions you're doing, whether that's social media posts or direct selling, you can speak directly to your avatar about your niche business. Have this person in your mind when you write your copy, speaking specifically to their wants, their pain points and how they want their problem to be solved by you.

The Price Is Right

Increasing your prices seems like a no-brainer if you want to increase your bottom line and see real cash in your hand. But many women get stuck with this and it can become a real obstacle.

Many female entrepreneurs have serious issues with charging what they're actually worth. They struggle with imposter syndrome and the opinions of other people. And that shouldn't be the case.

Your pricing should be reflective of your time and your target market. This should all come into play when you're actually thinking about how much to charge for your beautiful products or well-invested time.

No matter how you came to your current pricing I strongly suggest that you go back and take a close look at what your customers are actually getting from you.

If it's a service that you provide, are you considering:

- the time to reach your office space
- the overheads

- time researching before or doing paperwork after the actual time slot?
- The impact you actually have on your clients!

If you make a physical item, have you considered:

- the time you actually spend creating the product - how much do you charge per hour for your skill?
- the materials you use
- the tools that are required
- the design times
- the overheads?
- The impact you actually have on your customers! How well do you solve their problem? (I'm guessing it's a pretty big impact!)

The list goes on. So, tell me, are you really charging what you're worth?

If you feel uncomfortable with looking deeply at your pricing structure, you may need to go back and look at why you feel that way. Perhaps try increasing your prices by just 10% and see how that sits with you? How does it feel to say you charge that amount per hour? Per item? Say it out loud and sit with it for a moment.

If this brings up lots of issues for you, then I highly recommend that you also take some time to work on your money mindset. This is HUGE for many female entrepreneurs. You may want to pick up "Get Rich Lucky Bitch" by Denise Duffield-Thomas. This has been key in helping me to change the way I really look at myself, my worth and my business; and I know it will help you too!

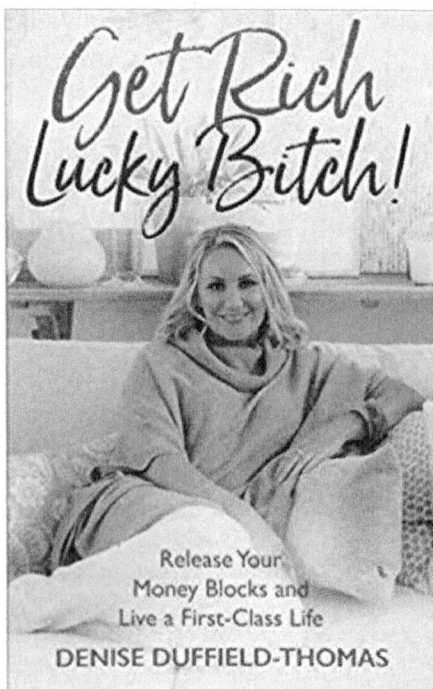

Get Rich Lucky Bitch!

Release Your Money Blocks and Live a First-Class Life

DENISE DUFFIELD-THOMAS

Generating More Money in Your Creative Business

We've covered the business basics and done the groundwork that will take you into developing a truly sustainable and successful business that's aligned to what you actually want. Now it's time to add new income streams into your existing business and promote the hell out of it!

An Introduction to Multiple Income Streams in Creative Business

You are a creative soul but, like we talked about earlier, you cannot physically DO any more than you're already doing. It wouldn't be smart for me to suggest you put in more hours to make more products or add to your already overflowing diary of clients. You may have more time available right now that you can fill with those additional creations, but how long will that last? And is that really sustainable? And is that why you started a business in the first place? Yes, you have the freedom of choosing your working schedule without the worry of sick days or flexible arrangements, but it's still specific when it comes to your income. The more you work, the more you earn.

The key isn't to work harder or for longer; it's working smarter. Changing the way you look at where your income is generated and how you do business. The ultimate goal: to diversify where some of the income in your business actually comes from. The more income streams you have, the higher your turnover and the more customers you can reach with the same time investment. Bonus!

JoelleByrne.com

What is Passive Income?

When you stop believing that you need to exchange time for money, at least some of the time, you can begin to generate revenue from streams that manage themselves. This is called passive income, and it's one of the best ways to get more cash into your existing business.

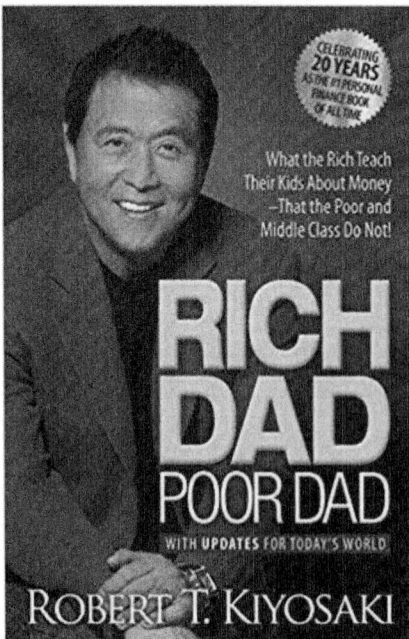

Passive income is certainly not a new concept. For generations, financiers have been insisting that the wealthy generate passive revenue by investing in property, stocks and high interest savings schemes. This is compounded in the bestselling book, "Rich Dad, Poor Dad", by Robert T. Kiyosaki, which made seemingly scary monetary concepts accessible to the masses.

The digital age broadened the horizons of passive income; with everyday business folks and hobbyists able to reach millions of people through the power of the internet. Not only has this revolutionised the way many do business, but it has also allowed millions of people to become entrepreneurs from the comfort of their own living room.

The Book, "The 4 Hour Work Week" by Tim Ferris, took entrepreneurship to the next level; allowing businesses to come alive and thrive on less than a full days "work".

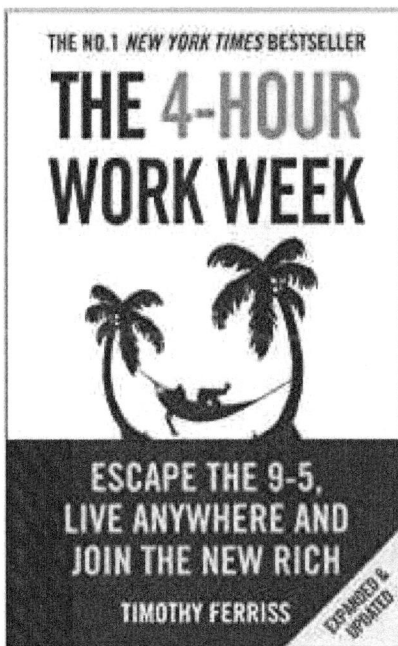

THE NO.1 *NEW YORK TIMES* BESTSELLER

THE 4-HOUR WORK WEEK

ESCAPE THE 9-5,
LIVE ANYWHERE AND
JOIN THE NEW RICH

TIMOTHY FERRISS

EXPANDED & UPDATED

How Can It Help You?

So, what am I telling you this for? Well, for starters, I need you to know that the way you've been doing business so far is not wrong. Far from it. If you were doing everything wrong, you'd have been out of business a long time ago. What I am trying to tell you though is that there are options for your existing business that you may not have considered.

The exchange of time for money does not have to be the "be all and end all" of your income. Your bottom line could consist of multiple revenue sources on top of what you're already creating. All leading back to a bulky bank account that leaves you impassioned to continue to create wonderful things with the time you do choose to exchange.

There are so many options for passive income streams that are relevant to your business. You are simply expanding on, or changing, the delivery of your specialist skill or knowledge. Create something once and let it produce revenue for you while you sleep. On autopilot! Or deliver your knowledge in a different way, reducing the hours spent labouring and amalgamating the audience.

Passive income is being paid for something over and over again, after the work is done. You invest an initial time and effort, for continued rewards that pay dividends while you work, rest or play. One of the best feelings is waking to more money in your bank account from sales you've made overnight!

Here are some passive income options you could consider:

- books
- Membership Programs
- Affiliate Marketing Promotions
- Drop Shipping
- Online Courses
- Investments
- High paying bank accounts
- Blogging
- Self-Publishing

Let's look at it more visually. Adding your existing product or service (referred to as "your offer" going forward) to multiple streams of income that all serve the same audience is an excellent way of creating AS MUCH INCOME AS YOU WANT, without worrying that there isn't enough time in the day to run all these businesses!

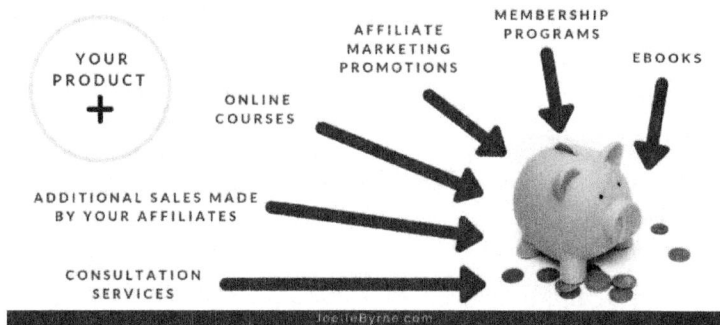

INCREASE YOUR BOTTOM LINE

Your existing offer + passive income = more money into your business

YOUR PRODUCT
+

ONLINE COURSES

AFFILIATE MARKETING PROMOTIONS

MEMBERSHIP PROGRAMS

EBOOKS

ADDITIONAL SALES MADE BY YOUR AFFILIATES

CONSULTATION SERVICES

JoelleByrne.com

There are also semi-passive income streams that you could consider. These can take a little more management than fully passive ideas, but are still worth thinking about, depending on what compliments your business.

- Teaching or grouping the delivery of services
- Rental Property
- Consultation
- Creating an affiliate program to sell more of your offer
- Flipping – buying in bulk, changing and re-selling items

Perhaps it's time to start thinking outside of the box for your own business?

JoelleByrne.com

Think of these. What:

- Might bring more revenue into your business?
- Passive income streams might work for you and your business?
- Skills do you share that others might like to learn?
- Complimentary products could you promote alongside your existing offer?
- Workshops could you offer that bring more than one paying client under your roof at a time?

The possibilities are endless, and this is just the introduction!

The key is to ensure that whatever you choose to add to your business, it needs to be relevant! You cannot risk alienating your audience by promoting products or services, under the umbrella of your existing business, that aren't in alignment with what you do as a business. That is business suicide!

If you do decide that you want to go into creating passive income away from your business, then that's great! Just make sure that if you are thinking of promoting anything on your website, social media or anywhere else linked to your existing business, that it is completely aligned with your businesses:

- Values
- Target market
- Branding
- Goals

Fail at this and you could ruin your business completely. Bluntly: It looks desperate. Don't do it. So, think carefully about what your business does, the service it provides and what compliments your existing offer without detracting from your business's overall values, goals, branding and target audience.
Here's an example (I do love my analogies!)

You run a craft business creating beautiful, handmade jewellery and decide that I'm awesome and you're putting everything that I've taught you into practice *wink*

The BEST complimentary services that would serve your target market include:

- Affiliate Marketing – promoting clothes and other accessories that compliment your jewellery style
- Drop shipping – Finding suppliers of products like jewellery cleaner and jewellery boxes to clean and store your beautiful

products in (these products could also be affiliate products)
- books – teaching your customers how to properly care for all of their jewellery products (not just yours) with step by step instructions on how to clean, store and treat their items (including within your guide affiliate links to other products that you'd recommend)

You may then want to consider teaching your skill. Know people who say how lovely it would be to be able to make unique pieces of jewellery that only they have? Teach them how!

- Write it down in an eBook
- Teach a local class of 5-10 people for one off or a group of lessons
- Record/film those lessons, add PDF worksheets and create an online course that you can sell over and over again!

I'd like to think that example got your creative juices flowing! I get very excited about the potential of unique, amazing women sharing their talents with the world and benefiting 100% from the cash and flexibility that can come with running your own business.

Introducing additional income streams into your business is so exciting with just a little knowhow.

Do it right, and you can take any goal that you set for yourself earlier and smash it!

Okay, so let's dive deeper into some of the ideas we've talked about above and let's get those money-making ideas flowing.

Become an Affiliate

What is Affiliate Marketing?

The idea of affiliate marketing can sometimes make people wince. It has an unfortunate reputation of being spammy and done badly in the past. That isn't the case. All affiliate marketing does is add products to your available stock without creating anything new yourself.

In definition, Affiliate Marketing is "a marketing arrangement by which an online retailer pays commission to an external website for traffic or sales generated from its referrals." That basically means that you sign up to a program run by a retailer who sells something you like or use, or something that would also be appropriate to your customers. You share these products or services via your social media channels and your own website, and then take a cut of any sales you make via your affiliate links. It's really that straight forward.

The retailer/advertiser (owner of the affiliate program) gets to make sales they wouldn't normally have made, through paying for advertising by you. The benefit for the retailers that run programs like these is simple; they only pay for the advertising that generates actual sales. Instead of forking out lots of cash for magazine ads, social media promotions and other similar advertising avenues that may not provide a return, they pay you AFTER a sale has been made.

You benefit because you're making a percentage of the profit with very little work in most cases, without having to create a product or service yourself. It's win win. And when you do it right, there is potential for matching or even outselling your current income stream from your business. It's that good.

Whatever it is that you're selling, there's ALWAYS accompanying items that would work well alongside your offer. Somewhere out there is a complementary product or service that would fit nicely with what you sell already.

Expanding your bottom line can be made very simple by signposting or recommending selected products or services to your audience that compliment your own.

For example, if you sell handmade jewellery like we discussed earlier, you might consider offers like:

- clothing lines to wear alongside your items

- jewellery cleaning products to keep your products in top condition
- storage solutions to keep your offers safe and cared for

See where I'm going with this?

In a nutshell, affiliate marketing, when done right, feels natural and authentic. It does not have to be "salesy" or scary. When you find the right products to promote, you can simply join the affiliate scheme and be paid a percentage of the sale price for every sale that comes from you.

Blending your existing business with affiliate sales expands your product range without you lifting a finger and provides a one-stop-shop for your customer base. Let's look at another example: You sell hand lettered wall art. Each piece is provided on thick, luxurious card. You get lots of custom orders, but also have a stock of popular quotes that sell well. As an affiliate you could promote:

- Complimentary frames for each piece; promoting different styles, colours and materials
- Complimentary wall paint, incorporating different colours that match your designs
- Complimentary furniture and furnishings

- Complimentary envelopes that those buying your offer as a gift could buy alongside your offer, in order to send it to the recipient

It's a big concept I know. But, once grasped, it's actually super simple and can have enormous returns.

Affiliate Marketing Does Not Have to Be Hard

The first thing you need to understand about affiliate marketing is that it doesn't have to be hard sell. I don't consider myself a natural salesperson and cannot think of anything I'd feel more uncomfortable with than spammy selling! If you get working as an affiliate right, you don't need to sell anything to anyone! The products and your writing/sharing style ensure these items sell themselves. You simply benefit from the passive income ticking into the bank each month. Then you know you are certainly doing the job right.

When I first started exploring affiliate programmes it was confusing. I felt like I needed to join every single programme available to me, whatever product they may be selling! Because they'd asked me to join their program, I felt like I needed to join and start to sell their products whether or not they were suitable for my niche.

STOP RIGHT THERE!

Not so much!
Understanding the promotions that would be suitable for your audience is key to ensuring that not only will you be accepted to these programmes when you apply, but you also make sales!

JoelleByrne.com is a blog about making more money from your existing business; if I started to flog you shampoo on my website and in my social media posts, you'd think I'd lost my mind (and I'd probably lose a huge chunk of my lovely audience who I'd like to keep – coz – ya' know…..)

To avoid this fatal error (and trust me, I've seen lovely ladies fall into this trap!) I'd suggest that you follow these few steps before diving into affiliate marketing:

Do Your Research

- Check back over previous blog posts or social media posts both on your personal pages and on your business accounts.
- Make a note of the products/ideas/services that you have been recommending?
- List these including the product/service and where it could be obtained from – i.e. is it a specific brand that you're promoting or is it a generic product that could be grabbed from general marketplaces like Amazon?
- Consider value for money and customer experience for your customers above everything else. Your audience trusts you to recommend the best product and experience. The worst thing you can do for your business is promote something that turns out to be crap! You're not legally liable, but morally…. Hmmm….
- Next ask yourself if what you've already promoted is suitable to your niche and audience? Are you selling the right things that solve your customers problems?
- Double check your niche market and make sure you've really drilled down. What are your customers problems? Find out their pain points (you should already know this to be running your business to the peak of its potential!)

Get with the Program

Finding whether or not a product or service has an affiliate program is as simple as Googling it! Literally type in "affiliate program for…." and insert your product/service.

If you know that lots of the items you'd like to promote are available from marketplaces like Amazon, then head over there and join!

You may need a website to join some programs. If you don't have one, and plan on promoting via social media then you have two choices:

1. pick a different program that doesn't require a website
2. create a really basic, free website using sites like WordPress, Wix or SquareSpace with a cover page that says, "website coming soon". Do this first, then apply for the program. You're much more likely to be accepted.

Where to Share?

Sharing your affiliate links is only limited to your imagination. The best and most lucrative places are:

- Your blog on your own website – creating evergreen content that can be viewed whatever the time of year that includes recommendations
- A shop on your own website – there are thousands of people out there making a full time living from only promoting affiliate products on their website. They buy a domain and set up a shop!
- As upsells – set up a "before you go" page, referred to in the industry as a tripwire, when someone checks out one of your products. This page thanks them for making a purchase and then suggests other items that will compliment what they've just bought
- To your email list – nurturing your email list is a lesson all of its own, but once you have developed the "know, like and trust" factor with your email audience, introducing them to products and services that will be of interest to them is a piece of cake!
- On social media – Facebook and Instagram posts tend to have more longevity than Twitter but test the water and see how you get on.

- On Pinterest – we'll talk about this in more detail at the end of the book!

Read the T's & C's

Ignorance is no excuse when it comes to joining programs and promoting affiliate links. You must declare that links are affiliate links, no matter where you share them. Depending which country you're in, the rules are different, so make sure you know exactly what you can/can't do legally.

Also, you'll be signing an agreement with a company, and they want you to make them look good too. They have a rep to protect just like you. Don't be a spammy pammy! Share links appropriately, with helpful insight and with a mix of other, non-affiliated content. Constantly filling your Facebook newsfeed with sales pitches does nothing for your reputation or the company you're promoting (this applies to selling your own stuff too!).

Be valuable! Provide so much good stuff, both free and paid for, that people can't help but love you! If they love you, they'll buy from you. It's that simple.

People buy people - I learned that from my amazing friend and mentor, Jules White. Check out her book, Live it, Love it, Sell it, for even more amazing insights into making sales part of your everyday life!

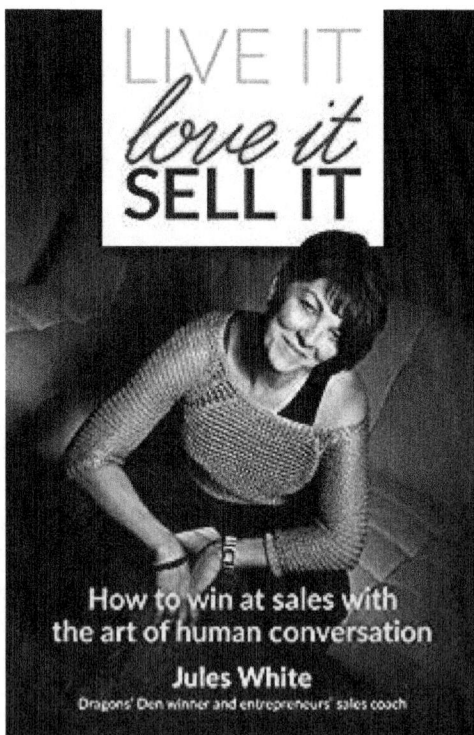

LIVE IT
love it
SELL IT

How to win at sales with
the art of human conversation

Jules White
Dragons' Den winner and entrepreneurs' sales coach

Two of the Best Affiliate Networks

Out of all the programmes I've tried, these two are the simplest and most lucrative platforms. I think anyone expanding their business online has enough on their plate without worrying about how things work!

These two affiliate programmes have helped me to make consistent monthly commission. I use links within my blog posts and social media without it feeling uncomfortable, pushy or completely out of place. These are brilliant starting points for anyone looking into affiliate marketing, whatever the niche.

ULTIMATE BUNDLES™

Ultimate Bundles (UB) are simply a pre-prepared library of curated content. Their products include eBooks, printable resources (planners etc) and courses that are grouped together under certain topics. They are offered at an exceptionally discounted price; up to 96% off the individual purchase value of each separate product. The bundles are usually only offered for a very limited time and often include great value bonus content for free.

Examples of some available now:
Photography Super Bundle 2018
The Ultimate Productivity Bundle 2019

They have different bundles running throughout the year covering topics from business and photography to parenting and home management. You can cherry-pick the appropriate packages for your audience, promoting only what is relevant and helpful to your readers.

They offer a generous, 40% commission on each bundle and affiliates do very well. Some very successful entrepreneurs and bloggers make ENORMOUS amounts of money with these flash sales throughout the year.

In addition to teaching you about the bundle's you can promote, Ultimate Bundles also provide marketing training before the sales go live to help you get the most out of your promotion efforts. They have a library of eBooks and video courses, constantly accessible, so you can scrub up on your marketing skills and etiquette any time.

The tools available to promote each bundle aren't anything to be sniffed at either! With images to download straight to your computer, html code for beautiful banners and text links for every aspect of the bundle, you're sure to get your audiences hearts pumping with brand-suitable and adaptable content.

Going from one product type to a world of brands available at your fingertips, Awin are a global affiliate marketing network that empowers advertisers and publishers (that's you!) of all sizes to grow their businesses online. They have over 100,000 active publishers promoting over 6000 advertisers (they're the brands!) which gives you, as a publisher, the ability to find and partner with brands you love.

Awin's aim is to help publishers big and small create profitable partnerships with the world's best-known brands through your social media, website, blog and content. They have a vault of brands to work with; whether your niche is beauty, electronics or finance, there is something for every style, brand and value available.

Signing up is easy and requires just a £5 deposit to ensure you're a legitimate prospective publisher. This is added to your account and refunded back to you once you're up and running. Once you're signed up, you can browse the brands available and pitch to those appropriate. You may also find brands approaching you to work together but, be picky! Don't forget your niche!

Once you're accepted to programmes, the process of accessing links and code is a walk in the park compared to other systems! From the affiliate schemes that I am a member of, this is by far the easiest platform to navigate and use effectively.

It is a very good site for finding appropriate banners of all different shapes and sizes if you want attractive links directly on your website or emails, because the navigation is super simple. Their process for deep-linking (converting a specific URL that you'd like your audience to land on) is very straightforward. You can also track those links with your own click reference, so you can manage and improve your strategy by analysing data that makes sense to you! A big part of affiliate marketing is understanding what is working, and what isn't, so this is a great way to start with that analysis process.

Awin also allows brands to find you! Interested brands are able to find and approach you to work with them in a few simple steps. You are then offered the choice of joining their programme or not, depending on your business plan and marketing strategy.

As a beginner in Affiliate Marketing, Awin is by far the easiest platform.

Summary

Joining any affiliate marketing platform requires filling out a form and you need information about your own brand and business to do this. If you're ready to monetise your online presence, this is information you must have available for all applications. I would recommend gathering that information as you complete the form by copying and pasting into a document. This will help next time you go to make an application, as you can simply copy the information across each time.

And for those of you worried about how to incorporate affiliate links into your own business – do it with value! Throughout this book I've recommended products and services that I know will help you! It's deliberate because:

1. The products are specific and relevant to the topic
2. They will bring huge value to my audience if they choose to do further reader or buy additional services
3. It provides a real example of how to seamlessly incorporate affiliate and non-affiliate links into your own work

4. I make additional income, at no expense to my audience, from a product I've already sold – double whammy.

So, there you have it; an introduction to Affiliate Marketing. It's pretty clear that promoting other people's products that are COMPLIMENTARY to your own, is definitely a way of boosting your business bottom line.

Community Over Competition

One of my favourite phrases in business is community over competition. This doesn't go down well with some business owners, but I genuinely believe that if you share your amazingness with the world, including your competitors, only good things will come of it. Because after all, there may be lots of people out there selling similar items or services to yours, but those people aren't you. You are unique, and people buy people when it comes to small business – not products! Embracing your unique selling point, your story and your individual skill within your business is a key way to stand out from the crowd and create a brand that people will know and love.

As part of the philosophy of community and working on the flow of complimentary products from earlier, there are a number of other ways to introduce passive income and beneficial marketing into your business through joint ventures and working with partners.

Similar to working with affiliate partners, looking to local and national companies to exchange services and mutually promote is a great way of offering additional products and services to your audience, whilst boosting your reach and your income.

JoelleByrne.com

Working with partners can be done in any number of creative ways, from recommending complimentary goods and services, to working together in joint ventures in order to bring real value to your customer group as a whole.

What about this for an example?

You make and design hand crafted products for weddings, including cake boards, guest books and table numbers. You could consider joining forces with:

- Florists
- Cake makers
- Venue designers
- Venue's
- Wedding planners
- Dress shops

Your partnership work could include:

- hosting your own wedding fayres
- offering group purchase discounts where, if a customer buys products or services from more than one of your businesses, they receive a discount

- promoting each other on your websites, social media and at events by carrying each other's business cards
- Setting up products or services that are exclusive to each other and offered only as a package deal
- Creating Joint Venture webinars or online courses that all parties contribute to and benefit from on a passive basis!
- Specific use discounts – where a customer buys your cake board and you offer the services of your cake maker partner at a referral discount rate
- Affiliate partnerships – as with the previous example, your cake board customer approaches your preferred cake maker partner for a cake. In return, you receive a previously agreed percentage of the sale.

You can get really adventurous when it comes to partnership work. The sky is the limit, because, depending on the offers you each have, you can use your imagination to tailor-make partnerships that benefit everyone equally. Whether it's a simple promotional tool, a local network generator or an exclusive group package – there's loads you can do when you work together!

So, start thinking about who you could work with to expand your businesses horizons. Be smart and make sure you have written agreements in place to ensure that everyone benefits from the partnership. You may also want to include an exit strategy too, so if it doesn't work out, all parties know how to move on without causing business disasters and having to split assets like a messy divorce! Ick!

Teach What You Know

Sharing Your Knowledge

Have you ever heard the phrase that "someone is always willing to pay for knowledge you have?" However small or irrelevant you think your skills are (they're not by the way!), there is always someone out there that would like to absorb that knowledge or gain that skill for themselves.

There are loads of different ways of recording the knowledge you have in your mind to share with the masses, from online courses or books (passive streams of income) to teaching face to face or running paid membership programs (active streams of income).

The benefits of online courses and eBooks is that once created, they sell through automated systems that aren't too difficult to learn. I use SendOwl to deliver my digital products and services, which is a simple and inexpensive platform with plenty of options for new starters.

This means that once created, the product you've made sells and your profit becomes "passive income" like we talked about earlier. These things will literally sell themselves if they're done right so you are no longer exchanging time for money. Kerching!

Have a think about complementary information you could provide alongside your current offer, service or product and the world is literally your oyster!

Could you teach a course that compliments your holistic service, write an eBook on enlightenment if you're a lightworker or run a membership program for jewellery makers?

Think about what you know and how it could benefit others. Most of all though, come from a place of service and your offer will fly off the virtual shelves!

Active Income Streams

Active income streams are still exchanging time for money but in a more efficient way. Once you've niched down to your speciality, it's possible to see a wider range of options of how you can deliver your product or service. The "big business" ladies I alluded to earlier are doing just this to increase their bottom line, whist exchanging the exact amount of time that they would have done producing one item or providing a service to one customer.

Some of the more active but better value activities you might want to consider include:

- Grouping products or services to deliver to more than one customer at once (specifically for service providers)
- Actively teaching your craft/skill in a workshop setting
- Attending relevant and niche events to network and sell your offers to the appropriate audience
- Offering consultation services based on what you do best in your business

These are just smarter ways of delivering a product or service and expanding the return you get on your time.

JoelleByrne.com

Let's say you're a Hypnotherapist: You work with one to one client's each day, and usually get booked out weeks in advance. You need to find a more time efficient way to deliver some of the knowledge and skills you share with your clients, whilst still earning similar, if not more at the end of the month.

You could consider the following Active Income Streams as a time saving, cash producing option:

Group Therapy - By creating group packages targeted at a specific issue, our therapist could introduce a group therapy service, where she can host up to ten clients in one sitting, for a set amount of time. Through researching the client base, our therapist found that issues like anxiety, stopping smoking and self-confidence are all very common themes among her client's issues. Creating packages that target and tackle very specific issues like this could bring in up to seven times the income from a one to one session. By charging less per session than a one to one appointment, but by including a number of sessions in one package that is payable in advance, our therapist can help more clients, in less time and generate more revenue.

An example of a package like this might be:

Anxiety Freedom Package

This comprehensive package is made up of:

- One to one appointment and initial assessment
- 5 weeks of group sessions
- One to one closing session and action plan to take away

Our therapist could highlight the pain point, include all the information about what clients can expect and the outcomes in one simple to create PDF document. The sessions would be at a set time each week, including options for daytime and evening workshops so she is not discounting potential clients due to their work/life commitments. Payment for this package would be in advance, and clients can then choose to turn up to sessions or not. If clients do not come to workshops, our Hypnotherapist isn't losing out on the income of that one client.

Another example might be - Holistic Wellbeing Workshops

An alternative, or addition to, the group therapy sessions is to provide wellbeing workshops. These could be sold to businesses as part of their personnel wellness packages, or to the general public who are interested in personal development topics. Our Hypnotherapist wouldn't need to spend too much time preparing for this, as she could tailor the workshops to demand or to the requirements of local businesses, charging more for bespoke delivery at workplaces.

Passive Income Streams

Teaching what you know from a passive perspective is just as simple and applies in a less complex way to service providers AND makers alike.

We mentioned on pages 24 & 25 about our jewellery maker, teaching her skills. Unlike the active income stream of group therapy sessions for our Hypnotherapist, our Jewellery maker can double her income with the click of a mouse. How? By providing an active workshop teaching setting, recording it and splitting it into bite-sizes videos. Add a few PDF files as aide-memoire's and Bob's your uncle! You have yourself an online course.

You could then go on to take screenshots of those videos, or create individual, step-by-step photographs, write down the information and create an eBook.

Your knowledge and skills are exciting, and someone out there wants to learn them! Applying your skills in a different way can be extremely lucrative, whilst sticking to your essential business values, goals and ideal customer objectives!

What Do You Know?

Many fabulous entrepreneurs underestimate the skills they actually have, and it's really sad. Your life skills and business experience are valuable and should be treated as assets in your business. If you're not a maker, designer or artist you can still teach what you know – look at me, teaching from my experience in working digitally. I hate to use myself as an example but it's important that you do really drill down into your skills and knowledge.

I am able to teach you today because:

- I have an in-depth knowledge of digital products, learned and implemented in a number of businesses
- I actively use and promote affiliate products in my businesses – therefore I know how it works, what works well and what doesn't work
- I have FAILED at business in the past! – teaching me what not to do so I can pass that information on to you!
- I have experience in writing, as once-upon-a-time, I wrote policy and procedural documents. Boring yes, but the skill I took from that was the ability to take a complex subject and break it down into steps, on paper

- I'm a ridiculously organised person – it's annoying to my family and friends, but damn does it help in business! I wrote down all the things I do to make sure my life is as simple as possible whilst being highly organised and bam, <u>book</u>! Passive income heaven!
- I have experience in strategy and planning – before I decided to work for myself and be a full-time entrepreneur, I worked in strategy and planning. It was my job to look at the bigger picture, find the problems and map out a plan of success. That's what I do now! Another skill taken and applied to my business
- Finally, I love meeting people and talking about ideas! And now, that's what I do every day!

So, you see, even skills that you underestimate as being part of "just your personality" can become useful and essential parts of building your business. You are a creative! Start using that creativity to understand the amazing parts of yourself that will help your customers!

An amazing example of making this work is Marc, who was highlighted to me on the Side Hustle Show recently. Marc made over $1.1 million dollars from his photography hobby.

But what's interesting is that he never:

- got paid to take pictures
- sold any of his photos
- held any photography workshops

So, what did he do instead?
He built (and subsequently sold) 3 websites related to photography, monetizing them by creating and selling digital products for photographers.

If you're interested in hearing how Marc knew what products to create, how he found buyers without having an audience of his own, and how he expanded this little hobby side hustle project into a serious income machine – check out this episode of the Side Hustle Show Podcast.

Smart Work & Marketing

Now you've added new income streams to your
business and considered the ground work, it's time
to pull it all together, get smart, make a plan and
take action!

Outsource Some of Your Marketing

Love it or hate it, marketing is a massive part of your business. Without it, you won't last long, and you won't make any money. And, to get it right, you really should do most of your marketing yourself. Why? Because you're the brand! People are buying into you AND your business. You are your own personal brand and therefore you need to show up to do your own marketing. Sorry!

BUT... and here's the good part... there are parts of marketing that genuinely rely on others around you. We all know that a good review, a share on social and a testimonial from a happy customer are literally worth their weight in gold, right? And, we've also talked about the benefits of partnerships, and working with the right people to promote your business. Lastly, we've also talked about how advertisers use publishers to promote their products for the best possible return, through affiliate marketing.

Remember:

The advertiser (owner of the affiliate program) gets to make sales they wouldn't normally have made through paying for advertising, they only pay when it generates actual sales. This is as an alternative to spending huge budgets for magazine ads, social media promotions and other similar advertising avenues that may or may not provide a return!

I actually know very successful entrepreneurs who run entire businesses based on affiliate marketing alone! It can be that powerful! They literally do ZERO promoting of their products themselves but reap hundreds of dollars' worth of sales every single day! This is through really smart marketing, which we'll talk about even further in the next chapter. But, for now, I want you to think about starting your own affiliate program.

Basically, this means having others sell your products on your behalf, according to your terms and conditions. You offer your affiliates a percentage of the sale price in exchange for their promotional services and you reap the financial rewards of sales you may not have made otherwise.

Having an affiliate program often means making sales that you otherwise wouldn't have made, to an audience you may not have had the pleasure of being introduced to. Some people balk at the idea of paying someone a percentage of their sale price, but you need to think of it as a sale you would not have made otherwise without your affiliate. Isn't 60, 70 or 80 percent of the profit of a sale better than no sale at all?

Affiliate promotions work, and you can only benefit by creating the details, terms and conditions of the program yourself! You literally get to tailor everything to how you want it to look!

I have my own affiliate program. My amazing affiliates range from influencers and bloggers with a great website presence, to crafters and creators who promote only on social media.

Because I have provided real value (and I hope you think so too!), my customers are happy to promote my products to their friends, fans and followers –

why – because they know that my ideas helped them and therefore will help someone else.

Your business is helping others. It's solving a pain point that no one else can solve in the same way that you can. You have satisfied a desire because you have happy customers. Why not pay those happy customers to sing even louder from the rooftops about you?

Platforms like SendOwl and The Passive Platform have simple to use navigation that allows you to start and manage an affiliate program very easily. It allows your affiliates to be kept in the loop with automatic emails that they receive when they sign up. Adding links to your products, changing your terms and conditions and deciding on the percentage earned for each sale can all be done with a few clicks of a button.

It will also work out how much to pay each affiliate and do it for you via your PayPal account. It couldn't be simpler, and this gets even more fun when your affiliates are promoting your products and services PLUS your new passive income products like courses and books!

Done right, affiliate marketing in the reverse can see you selling more of everything you're creating, driving traffic to your social media and website, and generally making you an all-round bad-ass that's helping customers in their droves!

1. YOU'RE ALREADY MY AFFILIATE - As a valued customer, you're already an affiliate for me; so thank you in advance! Find your affiliate links and a walkthrough of how to do it at joellebyrne.com/dashboard and earn 30% commission on every sale you make* (if you've bought a paperback copy of this book, simply email

hello@joellebyrne.com to activate your dashboard and receive a free copy of the eBook version of Creative Cash.)

*sales of all products excluding any paperback copies of books as these are provided by a 3rd party. The Passive Platform is limited to a 10% recurring revenue on sales.

Pin for Pro

When it comes to marketing, especially in the online world, we've got very stuck in our ways. There's lots to think about:

- SEO on your own website
- Content marketing
- Beating the algorithms on social media channels *eyeroll*
- Groups on Facebook, Instagram Pods and Twitter chats
- Other marketing like advertising, promotions and events

The list goes on! Being everywhere, all the time, in order to get noticed is hard! I know! But there is a clever little tool that most creative business owners aren't tapping into – and it's a mistake to ignore it.

Pinterest, along with Instagram, is one of the most visual platforms around. And most people think it's a social media site. It's not! It's a search engine. Consumers are more likely to go into Pinterest and make a purchase than any other channel! They go to look for ideas, inspiration and motivation as a solution to their problem.

You don't need to worry about algorithms, because with the right keywords and details, your pins can have life for YEARS!

And the best thing about Pinterest – you can literally bring everything you've learned in this book together to create a one-stop-shop of income-generating, marketing, awesomeness! IT'S THAT GOOD.

Pinterest allows you to:

- Reach massive audiences
- Target your market
- Be really visual in promoting your creative business
- Collect ideas that will appeal to your audience and serve them
- Promote your existing products or services
- Promote affiliate products and services
- Promote your new passive products and services
- Sell while you're sleeping, or eating, or whatever!
- Promote passive income streams in a passive way!
- Create content that doesn't disappear into the ether like it does on social networks

- Automate your pinning, so it becomes even easier to boost your business!

Here's a few tips to get you started on Pinterest, or to up your game if you've been letting it dwindle.

The main thing: Don't feel like you need to do everything at once either. Just go with the flow, and you'll soon start to see results from this amazing platform.

1. GET STARTED - Set up a business account or change your existing personal account to a business one.

2. BUILD YOUR PROFILE - Set up your profile so it clearly reflects your business. Include a title and tag line and complete the "about you" section using keywords and hashtags from your industry. Make sure to add a brightly coloured profile pic of either you or your biz logo (the more professional the better!)

3. CLAIM YOUR WEBSITE - If you have one, claiming your website gives you a more legitimate status for anyone landing on your page. Follow Pinterest's instructions to add the appropriate code to your website. (I promise it isn't that difficult!)

4. CREATE BOARDS -Aim for 10 boards to start with to make your profile interesting. Start by creating a "Best Of... (insert business name)" board. This will be reserved exclusively for your products & links back to your website! Create boards that have topics that are linked directly to your business and make sure to really drill down into the sorts of things your ideal client will be interested in. Don't forget to complete the details for each board, including the description with keywords and category.

5. START PINNING - Add pins to each of your boards by searching for keywords and clicking the pin button in the top corner. Aim for at least 25 pins per board to get you started. And don't be afraid to pin other people's content. Yours won't get lost I promise. On the majority of your boards, you need to be applying the 80/20 rule – where 80% of the pins are other people's and 20% are yours. (Other people's pins do include affiliate links though!)

6. DO YOUR RESEARCH - Follow similar boards and users that you come across, and look at what they're pinning, how their pins are laid out and what images work for your industry. Use Hashtagify.Me and pingroupie,

as well as Pinterest directly, to find keywords, boards and people to follow.

7. MAKE YOUR OWN PINS - Whether it's for a product, service or location, it's possible to create and upload a beautiful pin fairly quickly. Use Canva or picmonkey to create a basic, branded pin template, then reuse it, changing the image and titles. Include your business name or website on any pins you make to make sure they aren't "borrowed" by spammers!

8. SHARE - Upload your pin using the plus sign on the Pinterest app or desktop site. Include a link back to your website or the location of the product you're sharing. Complete the description using keyword rich text and hashtags. You can also use Tailwind to automate the whole process! Pinterest is a big driver of traffic to all of my websites, and I use Tailwind to take a lot of heavy lifting out of it. This is a serious part of my strategy and so, I invested in it from the outset and the returns are worth it. The income I make from affiliate pins alone is worth the small investment in Tailwind each month.

9. JOIN GROUP BOARDS - use pingroupie to search for boards based on your specific

niche or industry. Follow the board and its owner (always the first person's picture in the contributors) and then follow the instructions on how to join. No instructions? Drop them a message or email asking nicely to join!

Use Pinterest in a strategic way to promote everything including your physical products, services, passive products and affiliate products!

Consistency, Planner, Action

Okay! Phew! Well done for making it this far! I want to take the opportunity to thank you and to congratulate you. Only the women who take real action in their business can ever truly make an impact on the world.

So, this is just a little reminder that you're awesome. You got this. You can make your mark on the world, help people through the wonderful work you do and build the life you deserve as a result.

Now the soppy bits over, I want us to get into the final stages of the whole process. So far, you've built a little bit of a business plan to get you on your way. But one of the fundamental parts of business is taking the CORRECT action each day to see growth. Right now, we're focusing on monetary growth so that's what I'm concentrating on. But you can use this formula in ANY part of your business to make consistent steps towards achieving the goals that you lay out for yourself.

A business plan sounds boring and unhelpful. The sort of thing you create for a bank loan then stick in a drawer and never look at again. But actually, if it's done right, a good business plan is a map, a complete guide of how you're going to get from where you are now, to where you want to be. And if you don't know where you want to be, then go back to part 1!

So, I want to talk you through creating a business plan that will map out your journey from where you are now to reaching those goals.

1. Create a proper document

It's no good having bits of paper floating about with random pieces of information on it. You need to keep everything in one place. This can be as simple as using a Word or Google Doc or as tactile and exciting (to me!) as a beautiful new business planner or notebook. It doesn't matter. What does matter is that you have SOMETHING where all of the information, goals and plans that make your business, stored safely. (I recommend considering the Brilliant Life Planner by Brilliant Business Moms)

2. Write down your Niche information, target market and avatar

You need to know exactly who you are, who your business is, what you do, how you do it and who you do it for. Go back to part 3, Firm Your Focus, and make sure you are absolutely sure of all of this! I cannot stress enough the impact that it will have on your business! I was SO resistant to this and it held me back for years! Please don't make that mistake too.

3. Decide on your Values and write them down

Ensuring you know exactly what your values are is very important in business. They are very personal because they are reflective of you, your personality, your lifestyle choices and your morals! The values of a business give you the opportunity to state exactly what you will and won't do when it comes to your business. These values can be big or small, detailed or general – but what they will do is ensure that you can turn to them when the time comes for decisions to be made. And trust me, that time will come!

Here's mine to give you a taster of the sort of thing you should have in your business too:

JoelleByrne.com

✓ *Commit to integrity, excellence, honesty, transparency, innovation and creativity*
✓ *Community, kindness and karma over competition*
✓ *Go above and beyond – Make a difference*
✓ *Morals over money every time*
✓ *Empower people to hit their measure of success, whatever that looks like to them*
✓ *Keep the emphasis always on authenticity, choice, freedom and alignment*

4. Write down your goals

You wrote down a list of goals earlier and now I want you to make them proper! Get them written down in a format that suits you. Some people are more visual and prefer vision boards or images along with their goals.

Whatever you do, make your goals SMART - Specific, Measurable, Attainable, Realistic/Relevant and Time Bound.

Specific – What do you want, exactly? Do you know exactly what you want to accomplish with all the details? Goals must be well defined. They must be clear and unambiguous.

Bad example – more money
Good example - earn an extra £500 per month

Measurable – How can you keep track of whether or not you're meeting your goal? Can you quantify your progress so you can track it? How will you know when you reach your goal? Define specific criteria for measuring progress toward the accomplishment of each goal you set so that you can measure and keep track of your progress.

Bad example – more money (without knowing how much you're earning, exactly, right now and having no means of tracking it)
Good example – earn an extra £500 per month in addition to the £2000 I currently earn – tracked through an accounting app or spreadsheet

Attainable – Are you reaching so far that you don't even believe it's possible? Is your goal a challenge but still possible to achieve? Remember your Why/Why Not from earlier here too!

Bad example – Retire my husband next year
Good example – Retire my husband before his 45th Birthday (he's currently 37) so he can join me in working on our business, thus

increasing our income further and we can have more leisure time together

Realistic/Relevant – Similarly to attainable, is your goal realistic to your CURRENT situation and relevant to your life/business/other goals and plans? Realistic: Is your goal realistic and within your reach? Are you willing to commit to your goal? Almost certainly your goal is realistic if you truly believe that it can be accomplished. Relevant: Is your goal relevant to your life purpose? Your goal must be consistent with other goals that you have established and fit with your immediate and long-term plans.

> Bad example – Be a millionaire next year and retire
> Good example – Be a millionaire in 5 years' time and retire in 10 years' time with enough capital/passive income streams/investments/accessible pension funds to ensure I don't have to work again (then state how much that would need to be)

Time Bound - Does your goal have a deadline? Goals must have a clearly defined time frame including a starting date and a target date. If you don't have a time limit, then there is no urgency to start acting towards achieving your goals.

Bad example – earn lots of money
Good example – be a millionaire in 5 years' time

Implement ways to measure your achievements and track your progress each month. Don't get so lost in the big that you lose the little, awesome steps that take you there!

5. Break down your goals

So, we talked about this a little earlier, but now you have some additional ideas on how you want to increase your business income, you need to decide how and when you're going to do it. Going at it willy-nilly isn't useful and won't get you very far, very fast. However, if you make a specific plan based on your goals then your chances of succeeding increase tenfold! Here's an example:

GOAL – Make £500 additional income each month by May (let's say its January)
You need to think about:

- Where you'd like that income to come from? *Let's say you're going to create your own digital product, an eBook and also plan on teaching a group class at some point too.*

- Now break it down into how much you'll charge for each one?
  £10 each for the book and £25 per person for the class.
- In order to make your £500 extra per month, you can:

  - *Sell 50 copies of your book = £500*
  - *Sell 20 spaces on your group class = £500*
  - *Sell 25 copies of your book and 10 spaces on your group class = £500*

There's lots of potential here. Your only limit is yourself. Be realistic but push for more! Now you need to go on and plan HOW this is going to happen – it ain't magic!

6. Write down your action plan in fine detail

You now know exactly how you're going to create your additional income and meet your goal. The next step is to break that down into teeny, tiny baby steps that you can tick off one at a time! Start with the big steps and then break those down further.

Back to our example:

GOAL – Make £500 additional income each month by May

BREAKDOWN – Sell 50 copies of your book

BIG PLAN – Create and launch book

FINE DETAIL PLAN – including when you'll do this by!

Create and launch book:

- *Plan book content and write a synopsis – 15th Jan*
- *Write the content of the book – 20th Feb*
- *Plan launch marketing, events, social media – 1st Mar*
- *Find Beta readers to read the draft – 7th Mar*
- *Send draft to Beta readers with deadline – 14th Mar*
- *Research sales platform to deliver product – 21st Mar*
- *Create & schedule launch information – 28th Mar*
- *Receive reviews from Beta readers – 1st Apr*
- *Act on reviews & feedback – 14th Apr*
- *Build sales page onto website – 21st Apr*
- *Create a cover & mock-ups of book – 24th Apr*
- *Add reviews & images to sales page – 28th Apr*
- *Test EVERYTHING! – 30th Apr*

- *LAUNCH – 1st May*
- *Check stats, tweak social posts, be present! – all May*

Can you see how detailed your plan needs to be? Because if you say, "write a book" as your goal; it's big and scary and feels unattainable. But when you break it down into little steps (and go even further to plan each day!) you'll tick those steps off without thinking too much about it! And the next thing you know, you've reached your goal! Do this for every single goal and watch the achievements and successes mount up!

7. Be Consistent

If I've learned anything in the last 3 years, its that consistency is definitely key. You've got to show up, have courage in your conviction and confidence in your ability to do this. You can you know! Somewhere along the line you have built connections with people who have become your customers. You've created pieces of content from Facebook lives to blog posts to sharing a meme. You've driven people to get to know, like and trust you; which resulted in them buying from you.

If it's not happening right now then look back at the fundamentals, specifically your niche market. Keep up the work but don't flog a dead horse! Learn to recognise the difference between creating engaging content that results in sales and producing a few more double taps on Instagram.

Read your audience, understand them, ask them about themselves, engage, be you! But most of all, stick with it and show up. Consistency will help you to see what works and what doesn't. It will allow you to tweak the things that aren't producing the results and to scrap some ideas all together.

Have faith that you are needed in the world of business – because only you do what you do, like you do it!

What's Next?

You made it!

I'd like to think that you're closing this book with:

- A new zest for your business
- An understanding of some of the fundamentals that make all businesses do well
- A set of new and exciting ideas of how you can bring much more money into your existing business
- Goals that you want to achieve
- A plan of action to take you step by step to meeting those goals head on

If you don't have all of these things and need some help, you've got me!

Because you've purchased a copy of the paperback, you're also entitled to a free copy of the eBook version of Creative Cash. Simply drop an email to hello@joellebyrne.com with a copy of your purchase receipt and I'll happily send you a digital copy across! (This really helps when it comes to links etc!)

JoelleByrne.com

Head over to the shop and check out the other resources I have available that will guide you through the processes.

Need more than a manual? Want serious help and support from both me and a community of like-minded creatives? Join the Perfectly Passive Profit Academy (https://joellebyrne.com/ppp)

Want more? Come and find me on Facebook and join in the conversation. I'd love to know what you thought of the book too! Please leave me a review on my Facebook Page

Thanks for sticking around, and just shout if you need me! I'll be here… or in Costa…

Jo
Xoxo

Your Lightbulb Moments

This is your opportunity to write down all the awesome ideas you've had while you've been reading. Add links, hashtags, notes, brain dumps and all the other lovely ideas you've had to get more cash in the bank!

You deserve it!

Brain Dump Space

This is your opportunity to write down even more awesome ideas you've had while you've been reading… fill that space!

JoelleByrne.com

JoelleByrne.com

JoelleByrne.com

JoelleByrne.com

Printed in Great Britain
by Amazon